A STUDY OF WISDOM

A

A STUDY OF WISDOM

Three Tracts by the Author of
The Cloud of Unknowing

Translated into Modern English
with an Introduction

by

CLIFTON WOLTERS

SLG PRESS
Convent of the Incarnation
Fairacres   Oxford
0X4 1TB

ISBN 0 7283 0082 6
ISSN 0307-1405

ACKNOWLEDGEMENT

The cover picture, Jacob Summons His Sons, *is from
the Vienna Genesis, Purple Codex of the Sixth Century
in the Austrian National Library, Vienna,
and is reproduced by permission of the publishing house of*
MARIA LAACH ABBEY, WEST GERMANY

CONTENTS

CONTENTS

THE DISCERNING OF SPIRITS

INTRODUCTION

IN RECENT YEARS we have been rediscovering some of the riches of fourteenth century English spirituality, and they are circulating among an increasing number of readers. For the most part they have been put into modern speech which, while it may diminish the tang and edge of the original, does make their message more readily accessible. High among such classics is *The Cloud of Unknowing*, now widely read and appreciated. It is not generally known, however, that there are six other treatises from the same pen, shorter in length but of similar value and interest. Modern translations exist of three of these cognate works: *The Epistle of Privy Counsel, The Epistle of Prayer*, and *Dionysius' Hid Divinity*.[1] The remaining three, *Benjamin, The Discernment of Stirrings*, and *The Discerning of Spirits*, are here presented for the first time in modern dress. They are of considerable value, not only for the picture they give of medieval spirituality, but for their relevance for spiritual life today.

To date these seven works with any precision is virtually impossible. Though in effect they became public documents, in intention they were written to particular individuals, and at first were privately circulated. By their very nature they have no reference to contemporary events which would enable us to fix their place in time. The last quarter of the fourteenth century is as far as most scholars will go.

It is not easy to think oneself back into the circumstances in which they were first published. Their circulation and influence were limited by the fact that they were written and copied by hand. This in itself almost inevitably meant that sooner or later a copyist would make alterations or insert fresh matter to correct, expand or explain the manuscript before him. Authors had their works altered, bowdlerised, shortened and even plagiarised by others with little or no acknowledgement. Nor was the ascription of authorship any guarantee of its accuracy, for it was not uncommon for works manifestly not his

---

1. *The Cloud of Unknowing and Other Works*, translated into modern English by Clifton Wolters, Penguin Classics 1978.

to be foisted on a known writer, either to make such writings acceptable or in the pious hope of extending his teaching. This was so usual as not to attract attention or condemnation, and there are instances of it in the *Cloud* family.

The Cloud, for example, borrows Chapters 71-73 from Richard of St Victor's *Benjamin Major*, and derives much of its teaching in chapters 63-66 from the same writer's *Benjamin Minor*. *The Discerning of Spirits* depends very largely on a couple of St Bernard's sermons, edited with much freedom and with additional material characteristic of the *Cloud* style. The *Hid Divinity* is avowedly a paraphrased translation of Pseudo-Dionysius' *Mystical Theology*, and *Benjamin Minor*, one of our three books, is a classic example of this literary free-for-all. It is a vigorous re-writing of a much longer book of the same name by Richard of St Victor, from which our author has not hesitated to cut out a great deal of the original philosophising, and to touch up other parts. It is none the worse for such treatment, for it is eminently readable—more so than the original?—and preserves its essential thesis.

Of the *Cloud* books, *Benjamin* stands alone. Four of the remaining six are specifically letters addressed to individuals, unnamed but real, and a fifth has every appearance of being one also without actually admitting to the fact.

Letters on spiritual subjects have always been a marked feature of Christian religious writing from the times of St Paul and the apostles, and collections of such letters continue to be published from time to time. Although in most cases the writers, unlike Charles Lamb, are not 'writing for antiquity', there is plenty of evidence that some at least were aware that other eyes than those of the recipient would also read them. 'If any other be so disposed as thou art, to whom this writing may profit as unto thee, in so much the better, for I am well pleased' wrote the author of *Privy Counsel*, but he went on, 'Nevertheless, at this time, thine own inward disposition is . . . the point and prick of my beholding'.

The continual danger of this form of literature is that the reader may, albeit unconsciously, take the letters as written to himself, whereas the circumstances and the character which drew forth the originals can be widely different from his own. But if this identification is guarded against, much good can accrue. No one today is in the position of a Philemon to whom St Paul wrote in urgent haste, but the Epistle still remains a valid expression of the Christian ethic. The letters of Caussade to enclosed nuns are true in principle even for tycoons, given common sense.

AUTHORSHIP

The three tracts translated in this little book have always been associated with *The Cloud*. As with the other four there is no ascription of authorship, but there seems no reason to query the traditional view that they all come from the same pen, and that he who wrote one wrote seven. This is more easily asserted of *The Cloud, Privy Counsel, Prayer*, and *Hid Divinity* than of the three before us, for in *Privy Counsel* the anonymous author claims that he wrote them. But for the others tradition must be supported by internal evidence if we are to have any confidence in grouping them with *The Cloud*. Fortunately this is not too difficult because it can be shown that all seven share a common vocabulary and are consistent in the meaning they attach to words; they exhibit similar quirks of phrasing and display a restrained sense of humour which tends to tease when it does not deride the self-accredited theologian.

The style is both polished and sensitive, the work of one who is a master of his craft and an authority on his subject. This gives it a lucidity and directness which masks the great skill with which the points are made, for they are nothing like as simple as they seem. Dr Phyllis Hodgson, the leading authority on the text of *The Cloud* and its cognates, describes it thus: 'Here . . . is a highly complex prose, with an unusual variety of interwoven and interdependent clauses and phrases in numerous patterns, which leave an impression of sinewy strength and movement. The sentences are skilfully varied in length. It is suggested that their compactness is often the effect of a parenthetic clause or phrase, or of the substitution of a participial or prepositional phrase for a subordinate clause.'[1] She gives many instances of this treatment in all four books of the family. Probably, however, this stylistic richness

---

1. *Dionise Hid Divinite*. Ed. Hodgson, p.xlvii (Early English Text Society, 1955).

is due not so much to the deliberate application of verbal dexterity as to the unselfconscious artistry of a lively and disciplined mind which habitually thought and expressed itself in such ways. It is the same kind of cultured writing that was later to come to full flowering in the magisterial prose of the Cranmerian Prayer Book.

LEADING IDEAS

It is not merely language and style that link these three very different works; each of them in its own way and for its own purpose lays stress on certain characteristics of the spiritual life. Common to them all is an emphasis on the hardships involved, the sacramental direction required, and the discretion that is fundamental.

Hardships

That the way calls for a degree of real toughness is characteristic of all the *Cloud* writings. Basically it involves a determined effort to turn to spiritual account the various vicissitudes which will confront the reader. Among these are adversity—which has to be endured and conquered; the three-fold attack of the world, the flesh, and the devil—which must be resisted; prayer—to be offered faithfully and without ceasing; the doing of good, the life of quiet and patience, the acceptance of penance, the heeding of counsel—and much else.

But this stress on hardship sounds a deeper note which can lead on to contemplation. *The Cloud* is constantly underlining the 'work' necessary for its acquisition. It is not just a matter of facing trial and tribulation, but it is also the deliberate acceptance of the fact that God can only be approached through intellectual ignorance ('the cloud of unknowing'), so far is he beyond our capacity to understand, though not, of course, to love. There has, therefore, to be a serious attempt to put all human thoughts under 'a cloud of forgetting', lest they hinder the possible contemplation of God. If all this is endured out of love for God, this 'full great travail' is the complement and completion of the minor hazards of life, and together with them will produce the conditions in which God's 'beam of ghostly light' may shine more directly on the beholder, 'to ravish him out of mind'. In all the *Cloud* writings, this rich understanding of hardship and work must be remembered; sometimes explicit, sometimes implicit, it is always there.

Confession and Direction

Throughout his writings the author assumes that his reader will be regular in the practice of auricular confession and will submit to spiritual direction. In the fourteenth century penance was universally regarded as a sacrament and its use was firmly established. So long had this been the case that it was now held to be essential to salvation and the Christian life. In fact it had only comparatively recently—within the last three hundred years or so—become a *sine qua non* for spiritual health. Its practice prabably differed little from that of modern times, though (to judge from priestly text-books that have survived) the application of its benefits seem sometimes to have been more a matter of penitential book-keeping than would be encouraged today.

Spiritual direction is a natural corollary of such discipline. From the earliest times Christians have sought the guidance of their better-instructed and more experienced fellows. The fourteenth century Dominican, St Vincent Ferrer, summed it up when he said, 'He who has an adviser whom he obeys absolutely in all things will succeed much more easily than he could if left to himself, even if endowed with quick intelligence and possessed of learned spiritual books.'[1] While it is a widespread practice of long standing in the Western Church, it has never been systematized in the way that confession has. Indeed some spiritual guides—Benedictines are generally quoted as an example—tend to use direction with the object of dispensing with it, for the guide *par excellence* is the Holy Spirit, to whose leading in any case the soul must be always susceptible. As St John of the Cross wrote to the nuns of Beas, 'When one has made a soul know all that is necessary for its progress, it has no further need to listen to the words of others or to talk itself.'[2] It is doubtful whether the author of *The Cloud* would have been as liberal as this, at least to those for whom these books were written.

Discretion

The word suggests caution rather than excitement, a noetic rather than heroic quality. It is the power that discriminates, the insight that comes

1. *De Vita Spirituali* II,1.
2. *Letters* VI.

from experience, the balanced judgement that can decide swiftly and surely, the moderation and perspicacity distinguishing true wisdom from mere common sense. As with most virtues, some people seem more richly endowed with it than others, but all can acquire it because it depends for its fullness not on natural endowment but on divine grace. It has the further characteristic of being concerned with the rightness of things, unlike superficially similar gifts, such as sympathy or tact, which can sometimes suppress truth in the interest of avoiding unpleasantness.

Discretion was a highly prized monastic virtue, much esteemed by the Desert Fathers whose teaching was brought to the West by John Cassian (c.360-435). Indeed, Cassian is as good an exponent of the matter as any writer since, and the interested reader is referred to his second Conference, where Abbot Moses treats of the virtue at some length and with copious illustrations. The author of *The Cloud* has no doubt as to its efficacy and frequently refers to it. It has been suggested that his understanding of discretion developed with his own deepening experience of contemplative prayer. This could well be so, though it might be equally true to say that the variety of response elicited by quite different situations demonstrates the richness of his conception rather than a growing appreciation.

Thus in *The Cloud* itself the virtue is chiefly understood to refer to the ordering of one's life in whole-hearted response to God. In contemplation itself, there is to be no 'discretion', but all considerations of why and wherefore must be 'cast to the wind' (ch. 41). The problems which sometimes afflict the religious concerning food and drink, sleep and warmth, prayer and reading, are in comparison unimportant, and the solitary has to use his own discretion with regard to them. But he is not likely to go far wrong, if wrong at all, so long as he gives his whole attention to God and his call. Elsewhere in *The Cloud*, however, the virtue has a richer significance, as for example in chapter 54 where it is asserted that contemplation enables us to discern in the matter of social adjustment, so that a man can sense need, and read character, and be at home with anybody. In the same section of the book, much of which is devoted to the perils of over-literalism (chs. 51-68), the virtue lies behind and governs the reaction of the contemplative, even if the writer has no need to use the actual word.

In our three books the understanding of discretion is similar to that of *The Cloud*, while fresh facets are revealed by and in response to differing circumstances. The emphasis in *The Discernment of Stirrings* is on discretion as the outcome of experience, an experience gained after many falls and recoveries, and made fruitful by the grace of God. The picture we are shown is based on a text of Scripture where St James tells us that the man who has endured testing and has been proved will receive the crown of life (1:12). This crown stands for wisdom, or for joy, or for both. Wisdom is associated with discretion and the perfection of virtue, and these are typified by the gold of which the crown is made, the jewels that adorn it and the 'turrets' of fleur-de-lis projecting from its base. But the eagerness of his young reader must be tempered and guided by spiritual counsel and, by paying heed to his director, he will avoid many pitfalls and be better able to check his various urges. Instinct and upbringing contribute to the acquisition of discretion, but the infallible secret lies in the contemplation of God. He alone matters, and in the blind movement of love towards him is found the key to spiritual surefootedness.

The little treatise on *The Discerning of Spirits* repeats the theme. Its matter is rather different for, despite its title, it is primarily concerned with the sins of the world, the flesh, and the devil, and with those sins which spring from oneself. Discretion is essential if one is to distinguish the source of a particular sin. As always, contemplation brings peace, but if sin appears it has got to be put down promptly and firmly. To know the enemy's devices, to make use of the grace of God, to be firm of purpose and will, to pray and to accept counsel—all these work towards the the acquiring of discretion. And more than in previous works stress is laid on sacramental confession and direction, subjects on which the author writes with much 'sanctified commonsense'.

In *Benjamin*—'A Study of Wisdom' is its ancient subtitle—both Richard of St Victor and our unknown author are seeking to sketch the ways and means by which a soul attains discretion and is raised to contemplation. They achieve this by treating as an allegory the Biblical account of Jacob and his two wives, their two maidservants, and the thirteen children who were their issue. Jacob is made to stand for God, the women for different faculties, and their offspring and the order in which they arrive for the virtues that lead up to contemplation, typified by Benjamin. Once that is reached there is no further need for reason, for now the soul knows God and so, as in the story, reason (Rachel) dies. In the allegory the supreme virtue is discretion (Joseph), a gift much loved by God, as Joseph was by Jacob. But our authors are emphatic that this can only come after a long period of hard work and as the result of many a fall and uprising. And because discretion is the fruit of reason (Joseph was Rachel's son), so spiritual direction is essential, for it leads on to self-knowledge without which one cannot know God.

THE INTERPRETATION OF SCRIPTURE

In theory it is possible to distinguish between the Church and her scriptures, and to argue that the one could exist without the other. But in fact the relationship of the two is so close that Christianity's foes have sometimes seen the discrediting of the Bible as their best method of attack. Given a fundamentalist attitude to the written Word—and until the nineteenth century the Church was fundamentalist—it was not too difficult to do this. There are some tales, obscurities and myths that are indeed 'hostages to fortune', which pagan critics, from Celsus in the second century onwards, have not been slow to seize.

But the Bible has survived, and down the years has provided rich spiritual pabulum for learned and simple alike, despite the confusions so gladly indicated by its critics. That it has done so is largely due to the brilliance of Origen (c.185-254). In his book *Fathers and Heretics*, G. L. Prestige wrote of this great scholar that he recognised in scripture 'three distinct voices, the literal, the moral and the spiritual. The first of these is capable of being heard by any sincere believer, simple though he may be. The second is beyond the unaided powers of the simple' who, however, can understand the meaning once it is pointed out. The third, the spiritual or allegorical sense, 'touches profounder depths'. By using every effort we must strive to discover the vast underlying realities hidden by the literal sense, and make 'a synthesis between the genuine history and the spiritual fruits of allegory. . . The allegorical method "saved the Scriptures for the Church" ' (pp. 57, 58, 59).

Origen did not invent allegory, for pagan philosophers had long made use of it in their attempts to relate their idealistic hopes to the stark and awful world around them, but with Origen it broke new ground and took on sharper significance. For centuries afterwards, and throughout the Middle Ages, the Church handled her scriptures in Origen's three ways, whether in preaching or in written commentary. Everything had to be understood either in its literal, *historic* sense, in its *tropological*[1] (or moral) significance, or for its *allegorical* (or symbolic) value. Often the three methods would overlap or fuse, and when that happened to the tropological and allegorical they were sometimes understood to convey the spiritual or *mystical* meaning. Not many were content merely to expound the historical sense of any Biblical event, for it was always assumed as a matter of course to have happened, and the reactions of those present at the time were taken for granted. Expositors therefore concentrated on the moral or symbolic teaching.

The treatment accorded to the parable of the Good Samaritan will give as good an example as any. The fact that it is a story told by Jesus removes it from the realm of historical event, save that it was told at a particular point in time and described a tragedy all too common on the road between Jerusalem and Jericho. Inevitably therefore its interpretation will be along moral or allegorical lines. Our Lord himself did so expound it, with the tropological 'Go and do thou likewise'.

And some, not many, are content with this sort of exposition. We may instance the great eleventh-century exegete, Theophylact of Bulgaria, who by the standards of his day was very restrained and matter of fact. Thus: 'The Saviour makes known to us who our neighbour is, not because of his office or dignity, but because he shares the same nature as we do. Then be a neighbour out of love, and from a concern for him.' And when in the parable we learn 'it chanced a certain priest passed by', Theophylact simply remarks that some things in life happen without premeditation. Moreover, 'they [the priest and Levite] felt pity for the wounded man, I would say, when they became aware of him. But then, gripped by meanness, they went on their way.' It is only when the means of healing are being described that he begins

---

1. (i) *Tropus* (late Latin) = a figure of speech; -ology, the common suffix to denote 'the science of . . .' (ii) A moral and secondary sense of scripture.

to use allegory: 'To speak with men is "oil"; with God is "wine", which signifies divinity. No man can endure this latter unless it is blended with oil, with human association. "He poured in oil and wine" who saved us by his humanity and his divinity.'

But for most expositors such restraint was an impoverishment. The text contained far more riches. Our own Bede (*c.* 673-735), in his commentary on St Luke, and following his great mentor, St Augustine, found every detail important. The *certain man* is Adam, representative of mankind. *Jerusalem* is that heavenly city from whose blessedness he has fallen. *Jericho* is interpreted as the moon, and stands for this present changeable life. The *robbers* are the devil and his angels, *who strip him of his garments* of immortality and innocence. The *wounds* through which he would have died are sins, but he was only *half-dead* because though they had stripped him of immortality they were unable to rob him of reason. The *priest* and the *Levite* signify the priesthood and ministry of the Old Testament. Our Lord is the *Samaritan* who *binds up our wounds* by rebuking sin, and inspiring us with the fear of punishment and the hope of its forgiveness. *Oil* is penance, *wine* is warning. *His own beast* is the flesh in which he came to us, and in which he 'bore our sins on the Tree'. The *inn* is the Church of today. The *next day* is the post-Resurrection dispensation, and the *two pence* are the two Testaments.

Today most of us would dismiss this sort of exegesis as extravagant, but then we are children of our age, conditioned by the teaching that each parable has 'only one point of comparison, and that apart from this the details may, or may not, have a particular meaning'.[1] This is not necessarily the last word on the subject. Certainly no one in the Middle Ages would think Bede's exposition in the least ridiculous, but would rather wonder at the wealth of meaning to be found on every page of Holy Writ.

It was not thought necessary for each exegete to interpret the scriptures in the same way. Origen himself was prepared to accept five different interpretations of a text as correct in their varying emphases! The medievals exhibit much freedom. The popular story of Jacob and

1. *Oxford Dictionary of the Christian Church*, article under 'Parables'.

his two wives, Rachel and Leah, might seem to Richard of St Victor an admirable way to describe the developing spiritual life, and he so expounds it in his two *Benjamins*; but others referred the two wives to Mount Sinai and Mount Zion, Leah being the former and a type of the earthly Jerusalem, while Rachel stood for the latter, the heavenly city. (Cf. the anonymous *De Montibus Sina et Sion*, and Tertullian, *Adversus Judaeos*.) Yet others, like Commodian and Cyprian, use them to symbolize the supersession of the Synagogue (Leah again) by the Church (Rachel). Already in the second century Justin Martyr had claimed that 'Rachel is our Church' whereas 'Leah is your (sc. Jewish) people.' (*Dialogue* 134.2.) But St Bernard (1090-1153), in his turn is more sympathetic to poor Leah. His stress is on fruitfulness. 'You should not grumble at your Spouse for further gifts, for what he has given you —breasts full of nourishment for babes—is better and more needful than the wine of contemplation that you seek. For many are made happy by your breasts, while contemplation is for you alone. Rachel is the fairer certainly, but Leah is more fruitful.' (*Sermons on the Song of Songs*, ix.) 'With patience do I let myself be taken from the arms of barren Rachel, if Leah can make the fruits of your advancement to abound!' (Ibid, li.)

The fourteenth century—during which our books were written—was not generally expecting a Reformation of the kind that was going to burst upon it in the sixteenth. Nor could it possibly have anticipated the theories of Higher Criticism which were to come much later from Protestant theologians. Yet, for all their invincible ignorance in these matters, the medievals were neither naive nor simple, however much their outlook might be shaped by allegory and symbol.

Indeed, this is not surprising in an 'Age of Faith', for Christianity from the first has exhibited the same characteristics, though not perhaps to so great a degree. Our Lord's parables, the 'I am' sayings,[1] the Blessed Sacrament, and much else, are all expressions of truth under symbolic form. Some sort of allegory, broadly interpreted, is built into religious definition, and it is difficult indeed to see how it could be otherwise. Even a secularist culture uses symbol more than is generally realised:

1. St John 6:35; 8:12; 10:7; 10:14; 11:25; 14:6; 15:1.

a football team may 'slide into the relegation zone', a politician may 'let off steam', a hint may be 'dropped'—these and a thousand other expressions cannot literally be true, but they make abstractions concrete, and by the vividness of their parallels enhance our understanding. Certainly for medieval man the use of the symbol enriched his knowledge of life. Not for him the possibility of psychologising or philosophising in twentieth-century fashion, but he looked at life no less shrewdly and intelligently. By means of allegory he saw man in the round, and often enough was able to add a fourth dimension because of the insight it gave. He would reckon it absurd to think that the meaning of anything, animate or inanimate, if it had been created by God and was being sustained by him, had to be restricted to its particular function in the world of phenomena. The most ordinary life had significance beyond its immediate situation, for it could stand for (and often did) a greater reality 'written in the heavens'. Everyman was potentially a cosmic figure, living on the background of eternity. Always there was more in life than met the eye. 'Now we see through a glass darkly'; but even so everything, by the very fact of its being what it is, is symbolic of something more.

This way of looking at life had many facets. Sometimes the symbols were arithmetical, based on the cycle of the year. The four seasons spoke of the four evangelists, the twelve months of the twelve apostles. The seven days of the week were richly evocative: the seven virtues, the sevenfold gift of the Holy Spirit, the seven Beatitudes, the seven petitions in the Lord's Prayer, the seven sacraments, the seven deadly sins, the seven penitential psalms. It was the perfect number. Often the parallel was more obvious. Take colour: red is the colour of blood, Christ's blood, so red roses portrayed sacrifice and martyrdom. White is the colour of purity, so white roses signified virginity and beauty. But roses have thorns, and they entail suffering.

Strict allegory was often ingenious and cleverly worked out. The scriptures, domestic life, the animal kingdom, history, legend, were all pressed into service. Not all the allegories were religious in their application. Some were social documents, some anti-clerical, some satirical. Perhaps the most famous is Langland's *Piers Plowman*, but there are others, notably by Chaucer, which are also read today. Whatever their origin, they invested people and things with significance beyond the immediate present, and they showed man to be a creature of high destiny and value—in no sense a figure of straw or a mere unit.

In the three books before us we find examples of allegory, analogy and symbol. *Benjamin* is sufficient illustration of the first, and no one would think the story of Jacob and his wives incapable of bearing a richer and more spiritual meaning. In *Stirrings* we have the analogy between the weather and sea confronting the traveller and the experiences awaiting the would-be contemplative. In the same tract there is a splendid specimen of symbol supplied by the royal crown, its texture and shape, which speak of the virtues inherent in the crown of life. The *Discerning of Spirits* has a brief comparison between the shriven soul and a clean sheet of paper. In all these uses of allegory, analogy and symbol, as well as in the homeliest figures of speech, our unknown author invites the humble reader in search of wisdom to contemplate their deeper implications.

*   *   *   *   *   *

This translation is based on the British Museum manuscript, Harleian 674, generally reckoned to be the best of the existing *Cloud* MSS. It owes much to the helpful suggestions of three people in particular, my wife, and Sister Edmée and Sister Isabel Mary of the Community of the Sisters of the Love of God. They have eliminated many infelicities and have tidied it up in various places. Mrs Mildred Mudie of Newcastle Cathedral was responsible for the bulk of the typing. To all of them special thanks are due.

C. C. W.

BENJAMIN

A Tretyse of the Stodye of Wysdome
that men clepen
Benjamin

BENJAMIN

Introduction

AS WE have seen, this treatise is a rewriting by our author of the much longer work called *Benjamin Minor* by Richard of St Victor. Very little is known about this key figure of medieval spirituality. He was a Scot, and a religious of the great Parisian Abbey of St Victor, famed for its piety and learning. He was a man of parts, for he was an outstanding theologian, philosopher, psychologist, expositor and mystic. He wrote at least forty-two treatises on various subjects, of which the best known are probably his *Benjamin Minor* and *Benjamin Major*. They are still very readable. He died in 1173, apparently in the prime of life. His teaching pervaded much mystical theology in Western Christendom, and is one of the formative influences behind *The Cloud* family of writings.

In seeking to describe spiritual states Richard was writing in a period of transition. Until his day authors had not ventured much beyond scriptural exegesis, however remote from its obvious meaning might be the particular gloss they put on Holy Writ. But other styles were on the way, and already the Schoolmen were analysing, defining, and describing spiritual and mystical experience with an accuracy and clarity unattainable by the earlier methods. Though its full flowering was yet to come Richard is not unaffected by such an approach, for he handles his texts with considerable freedom, often using them as pegs, and no more, on which to hang his psychological judgements. By the time we get to his most important work, *Benjamin Major*, this treatment has developed even further, and the link with scriptural interpretation is often sketchy to the point of non-existence.

The argument is a fascinating specimen of medieval allegorizing. It uses the eighteen characters of Jacob's domestic life to point the steps towards contemplation. The story of the patriarch is set out in Genesis, chapters 29-50, and tells how Jacob becomes the father of thirteen children by his two wives, Leah and Rachel, and their two maidservants,

Zilpah and Bilhah. In the symbol Jacob himself stands for God, while the rest are virtues which develop in the contemplative soul. It is all very neatly worked out and, given the background of the day, plain for all to see.

None of today's Biblical critics would accept it, of course. By a process of speculation no less intriguing than the medieval, but possibly more accurate, they see in this particular Jacob saga the symbolic account of the entry of Semitic tribes into Egypt, and in the rivalry of the two wives and their handmaids, two waves of immigration each comprising six tribes apiece. The theories underlying this reconstruction are themselves confused and sometimes conflicting, and the interested reader should turn to the learned commentaries for further enlightenment.

In the time of Richard of St Victor the Vulgate version of the Bible was in a somewhat defective form and it is not therefore always possible to trace to their source some of his interpretations. Richard's use of the Hebrew names is based on the interpretations given by St Jerome and St Isidore in their Etymologies and by St Gregory the Great in his Commentaries.[1]

---

1. See the Introduction and Notes by Clare Kirchberger to her translation of *Richard of Saint-Victor: Selected Writings on Contemplation*, London 1957.

A TREATISE OF THE STUDY OF WISDOM
THAT MEN CALL
BENJAMIN

Prologue

A GREAT theologian, Richard of St Victor, in one of his books about the study of wisdom, asserts that there are two faculties in man's soul, and that they are put there by our heavenly Father from whom all good comes. One is *reason*, the other *affection* or *will*. Through reason we know, through affection we feel or love. From reason comes sound advice and inward perception, and from affection spiritual desires and ardent emotions.

Just as Rachel and Leah were the two wives of Jacob, so, in a not dissimilar way, man's soul, both through the light brought by knowledge, and through the sweetness of love that comes with affection, is espoused to God. Jacob symbolises God, Rachel reason, Leah affection. Each of these wives had a maidservant: Rachel had Bilhah, and Leah Zilpah. Bilhah was a great chatterbox, while Zilpah was always drunk or thirsty. Bilhah, Rachel's servant, represents *imagination*, which is servant to reason. Zilpah stands for *sensuality*, which serves affection just as she served Leah. And these servant girls were so essential to their mistresses that, had the whole world been at their disposal, without them it would have been of no use at all. Outward, bodily things cannot be known by reason without the help of imagination, and without sensuality affection is unable to feel them. And yet imagination in her ignorance cries out so loudly in our soul's ears that, however hard she tries, her lady, reason, cannot silence her. Thus it often happens that when we are wanting to pray, so many varied, fantastic and bad thoughts are crying out in our hearts that we are unable to drive them out despite our every effort.

It is evident from this that, symbolically, Bilhah is foul-mouthed, and that sensuality, Zilpah, is always so thirsty that for all the affection her mistress lavishes on her she is unable to slake her thirst. Why, the whole world is not enough to meet sensuality's appetite! In much the same way it happens sometimes that, when we are praying or thinking about God and spiritual matters, and want to feel the sweetness of love in our affection, we are unable to do so because we are absorbed in attending to the greed of our sensuality. It is aways greedily asking, and our flesh sympathises with it. Clearly Zilpah is forever drunk and thirsty!

And just as Leah, through Jacob, conceived and bore seven children, and Zilpah, Bilhah and Rachel two each, in a similar way affection, through the grace of God, bears and produces seven virtues, and sensuality, imagination and reason two virtues or perceptions each.

The names of these children and their corresponding virtues can be classified thus:

i The husband, who is Jacob, represents *God*.

ii The wives are Leah, who stands for *affection*, and Rachel, who represents *reason*.

iii Leah's servant is Zilpah or *sensuality*, and Rachel's is Bilhah or *imagination*.

iv Jacob and Zilpah have two sons: Gad (*abstinence*) and Asher (*patience*).

v Jacob and Leah have seven sons: Reuben (*fear of God*), Simeon (*sorrow for sin*), Levi (*hope of forgiveness*), Judah (*love of God*), Issachar (*joy of inner sweetness*), Zebulon (*perfect hatred of sin*), Dinah (*proper shame of sin*).

vi Jacob and Rachel have two sons: Joseph (*discretion*), and Benjamin (*contemplation*).

vii Jacob and Bilhah have two sons: Dan (*awareness of future judgment*), and Naphtali (*awareness of future joy*).

In this scheme we have set out Jacob and his wives, their servants and all their children. We now intend to show how the children came and in what order.

First, we must speak of Leah's children, for we read that she was the first to conceive. The sons of Jacob and Leah stand for the lawful affections or feeling in man's soul; were they improper they would not be his sons. Moreover, Leah's children stand for the same number of virtues, for virtue is no more than a right and proper feeling in our soul.

We can say a soul's feeling is right when it relates to what it ought to be, and is proper when it has attained its fulfilment. Feelings can be right and proper, and sometimes wrong and improper. When they are the former, they can be counted among the sons of Jacob.

I

How the virtue of fear arises in the affection

Leah's first child by Jacob was Reuben or *fear*. It is written in the Psalms that 'the fear of the Lord is the beginning of wisdom'. (111:10; 19:9.) This is the first virtue to be felt in a man's affection and without it no other virtue can exist. So whoever wants to have fear as his son must consider seriously and often what evil he has committed. On the one hand he must recall the greatness of his sin, and on the other the power of his Judge. From such reflections fear is born: in other words, Reuben, who is rightly called in addition *the son of perception*. For that man is truly blind who cannot envisage the punishment to come, and in consequence is not afraid of sinning. Reuben is well called the 'son of perception', for when he was born his mother cried, 'the Lord has looked upon my affliction'. It is by such recollection of past sin, and the Judge's power, with the resultant feeling of fear, that a man's soul really begins to see God and, in his merciful pity, to be seen by God.

II

How sorrow arises in the affection

While Reuben is growing Simeon is born, for sorrow necessarily follows close upon fear. It is a fact that the more a man fears the punishment he deserves, the more deeply he sorrows for the sin he has committed. Leah in giving birth to Simeon cried out, 'Because the Lord has heard that I was hated he has therefore given me this son'. Which is why

Simeon is also called *hearing*, for when a man is deeply sorry and despises his old sins he begins to be heard by God and, what is more, to hear God himself utter this blessed word, 'Blessed are they that sorrow, for they shall be comforted.' (Matt. 5:4.) And when a sinner is sorry and turns from his sin he is safe. The Bible says this. Humbled with Reuben, he is contrite with Simeon, in sorrow and tears, just as David says in the Psalms, 'a broken and contrite heart, O God, thou shalt not despise'. (51:17) Without doubt such sorrow brings true consolation.

III

How hope arises in the affection

But I want to know what comfort can there be for those who have a genuine fear and a deep regret for their past sins, if there is no real hope of forgiveness?

This is where the third son of Jacob comes in. In the story Levi is called *added*, for when the two other children, fear and sorrow have been given to a man's soul by God, this third one, which is hope, will surely not be far behind. What is told us about Levi confirms this, for after his brothers Reuben and Simeon had been given to their mother Leah he, Levi, was added.

Notice that the word is 'added', not 'given'. It is in order that a man should not take the hope of forgiveness for granted until his heart has been humbled by fear and made contrite through sorrow. Without these two hope would be presumption, but where they are present it is added to them. So after sorrow comes a degreee of comfort, as the Psalmist David says, 'In the multitude of the sorrows I had in my heart, your comforts have refreshed my soul.' (94:19.) This is why the Holy Spirit is called the Paraclete, or Comforter, for often he will grant comfort to a sorrowing soul.

IV

How love arises in the affection

From now on an increasing intimacy develops between God and the soul, a kindling of love, so to speak. A man often feels that he is being visited by God, and indeed he is much cheered by his coming. Leah first felt this growing loving familiarity after the birth of Levi when she called out exultantly, 'Now will my husband be joined with me'. The true husband of our soul is God. And we too are joined to him in fact when we draw near him by hope and true love. But love is the result of hope, and so Judah is born after Levi, the fourth son of Leah.

When she was giving birth to him Leah cried, 'Now will I praise our Lord'. And so in the story Judah is called *praise*. Before a man feels this love in his soul, everything he does is done more out of fear than out of love. But in this new phase his soul feels God to be so sweet, merciful and good, so courteous, true and kind, so faithful, loving and intimate,[1] that there is nothing in himself—his strength or mind or will— that he does not offer deliberately, freely and completely to him. He confesses not only his sin, but the goodness of God. It is a great proof of love when a man tells God he is good. David often mentions this confession of praise, as for example when he says, 'Make it known to God that he is good'.[2]

We have spoken now of four of Leah's sons. For a while after this she stopped bearing children. And a man's soul tends to think it has all it needs when it loves real goodness. Indeed it is enough for salvation, but not for perfection, because the perfect soul needs not only to be inflamed with the fire of love in its affection, but to be illumined too by the light of knowledge in its reason.

---

1. 'Curteis' (courteous) and 'homely' (intimate) are key words of Mother Julian.
2. cf. Pss. 86:5, 106:1, 119:68, etc.

V

How the twofold sight of pain and joy arise in the imagination

So when Judah has been born—that is to say, when love and a longing for good (no less real for being unseen) has sprung up and is growing in the affection—it is Rachel's turn to want to bear children. In other words, reason is now anxious to understand what it is that affection is experiencing. For just as it belongs to Leah, *affection*, to love, so it belongs to Rachel, *reason*, to know. From Leah, *affection*, spring feelings which are right and proper, and from Rachel, *reason*, knowledge and understanding that is accurate and lucid. And the more Judah, *love*, grows, the more does Rachel want to bear children. To put it differently, reason strives to understand.

Surely there is no one who does not realise how hard it is for the mind of the flesh, unversed as it is in spiritual matters, to attain to the knowledge of invisible things, and to contemplate things spiritual? It is virtually impossible, because the soul that is 'fleshly' and ignorant is aware of nothing but physical matters, and its mind can only think of the things it can see. All the same it does its best to look within itself, and what it cannot see clearly by spiritual knowledge, it thinks it sees by using its imagination.

And this is the explanation of Rachel's having children through her servant before she had them herself. For though a man's soul may not yet have the light of spiritual knowledge in his reason, he still thinks it sweet to stay his mind on God and spiritual things by using his imagination. Just as we take Rachel to represent reason, so by Bilhah, her servant we understand *imagination*. So reason shows that it is more worthwhile to think of spiritual things in whatever way possible—for example in the kindling of desire by some imagined beauty—than it is to think of vain, false and worldly things. Therefore Bilhah bears two sons, Dan and Naphtali. Dan signifies *the awareness of future punishment*, and Naphtali *the sight of future joys*.

Both these children are necessary, for they profit the active soul, one by putting down all sinful suggestions, and the other by stimulating our will to do good, and by kindling our longing. For just as it is Dan's business to suppress evil and sinful promptings by considering future punishment, so it is the function of the other brother, Naphtali, to spur our wills on to do good and to stir up holy desires by the sight of joys to come. Thus, if and when saints are moved to do something improper (as for instance when some foul thought arises) at once they picture to themselves the future suffering, and so nip the temptation in the bud, before it produces any evil delight in the soul. And whenever their devotion and love for God and spiritual things weaken and grow cold— it often happens in this life because of our corrupt flesh, and for other reasons too—they give themselves to consider the joys to come. Thus they fire their will with holy desires, and destroy temptation at the outset, before it can make them sluggish and depressed.

And because we, like Dan, condemn all improper thoughts, the story calls him *judgement*. Jacob his father said, 'Dan shall judge his people'. The story also tells us that when Bilhah gave birth to Dan, Rachel said, 'God has judged me'. That is to say, 'the Lord has made me equal to my sister Leah'. And this is just what reason says when imagination has caught a glimpse of future punishment, that the Lord has made her equal to her sister, affection. She was only able to say this because she had seen the future punishment in imagination, and she was already afraid of it, and feeling sad.

And then comes Naphtali, *the sight of future joy*. When he was being born Rachel said, 'I have been made like my sister Leah', and so in the story Naphtali is called *likeness*. And reason claims she is like her sister affection, because though the latter knew, and could feel, hope and love for the coming joys, she, the former, has caught a glimpse of it in her imagination. Jacob described Naphtali as 'a hind let loose: he gives good words'. For this is the effect when we imagine the joys of heaven. For Naphtali quite wonderfully inflames our soul with holy desires whenever we imagine the splendours and beauties of heaven.

VI

How the virtues of abstinence and patience spring up in sensuality

When Leah saw how delighted Rachel was at the birth of her servant
Bilhah's two bastard sons she summoned her own servant Zilpah to lie
with her husband that she in her turn might rejoice by having two
more infants through Zilpah. A man's soul is not unlike this, for once
reason has begun to control the wayward imagination and has made
her obedient to God and fruitful in assisting knowledge, so too does
affection control the lusts and thirsts of sensuality, by making her also
obedient to God, and thus fruitful in assisting her feeling.

But what fruit can she bear if it is not by learning to live modestly
when things go well and patiently when they go ill? Zilpah's children
are Gad and Asher, Gad standing for *abstinence* and Asher for *patience*.
Gad was born first and Asher second. For it is essential that we first discipline ourselves by sensible abstinence, and afterwards endure life's
discomforts in the strength that patience gives. These are the children
that Zilpah bore in sorrow, because through abstinence and patience
sensuality suffers greatly in the flesh.

But what is sorrow to the senses turns to great joy and happiness
in the affection. For example, when Gad was born, Leah cried out,
'Happy!', which is why Gad in the story is called *happiness* (or *blessedness* if you prefer it). And so we say, quite rightly, that abstinence in
sensuality means bliss in affection. It is always true that the less sensuality delights in lust the more does affection experience sweetness in
her love.

Again, when Asher was born Leah said, 'This means bliss for me',
which is why the story calls Asher *blessedness*. And so we can properly
go on to say that patience in sensuality also means bliss in affection.
For the greater the difficulties sensuality has to put up with, the greater
is the soul's blessedness in the affection.

When we speak of abstinence and patience we are not only thinking
of moderation in food and drink, or enduring outward troubles, but
also of coping with every kind of delight—carnal, natural, worldly—and

every kind of hardship, physical or spiritual, within or without, reasonable or inexplicable, and with things which please our five senses, or which torment our sensuality. In this way sensuality produces the fruit that helps her mistress, affection. Much peace and rest does the soul know that refuses to yield to sensuality's lusts, or to complain of its difficulties. The first of these comes through Gad, the second through Asher.

At this stage we ought to consider why Rachel's servant received Jacob before Leah's did. The reason is this: if we did not first control our turbulent imagination and those intrusive and wild thoughts, there can be no doubt that we would be quite unable to moderate the lusts of sensuality. So he who wishes to abstain from carnal and worldly desires must seldom or never think vain thoughts. In this life it is never possible for a man to despise carnal comforts completely or to meet hardship unafraid until he has thoroughly considered the rewards or torments that lie ahead of him.

Now we can begin to understand how, with these four sons of these two servant women, the citadel of our conscience is kept so wonderfully in all its temptations. Temptation arises either from within, in our thoughts, or else from without, through one of our five senses. Those within have Dan for judge, and he quenches evil thoughts by showing us the punishment; those coming from outside find that Gad sets the practice of abstinence against such evil delights. Dan watches over the interior, Gad the exterior. And their two brothers afford them much help: Naphtali makes peace along with Dan, and Asher tells Gad not to be afraid of his enemies. Dan frightens us with the horrors of hell, while Naphtali comforts us with the bliss of heaven. Asher also helps his brother outwardly, so that through the help of them both, the walls of the citadel remain intact. Gad proffers comfort, Asher dismisses discomfort. Asher at once attacks his enemy by summoning his characteristic patience, and the promise symbolised by Naphtali. The more enemies he has, the more opportuniity he has for success. So when he has overcome his foes (the adversities of the world) he immediately turns to help brother Gad destroy them. Whenever he appears they inevitably turn tail and flee. Gad's enemies are carnal pleasures. But in truth, from the day a man learns patience through the discipline of abstinence, false pleasures find no resting place.

VII

How the joy of interior sweetness arises in the affection

So when the enemies have flown and the citadel is at peace, a man can experience the deep peace of God, the peace 'that passes understanding' (Phil. 4:7). The reason is that Leah bore no more children until after her servant Zilpah had borne Gad and Asher. For it is a fact that if a man has never subdued the evil lusts of his five senses through abstinence and patience he will never feel in his affection any inner sweetness, or have true joy in God and spiritual things. This is why Issachar, Leah's fifth son, is called in the story *reward*.

This joyful interior sweetness is well called 'reward' for it is a foretaste of that heavenly bliss which is the eternal reward of the devout soul; and it begins here below. When Zilpah gave birth to this child, Leah said, 'God has given me my reward because I gave my slave girl to my husband to bear children'. It is good when we make our sensuality fruitful by abstaining from carnal and worldly comfort, and when we endure carnal and worldly hardships. For then in his great mercy our Lord gives us unspeakable joy and interior sweetness in our affection, a foretaste of the supreme happiness and reward awaiting us in the kingdom of heaven.

Jacob described Issachar as a 'strong ass living between two extremes'. A man in this state who experiences the earnest of that everlasting joy is indeed like a strong ass living between two extremes, for however full he may be of spiritual and joyful happiness in God, the corruptibility of his mortal flesh obliges him to exercise care for his dying body, with its hunger and thirst and other discomforts. Hence the parallel between 'ass' and 'body'. In soul he is strong; he can destroy all carnal passion and lust through patience and abstinence in sensual matters and also by the abundance of sweet and spiritual joy known in his affection. Such a soul dwells between the two extremes of life, mortal and immortal, and he who lives between such limits has almost forsaken mortality—but not quite! And he has almost attained immortality—but, again, not quite! For as long as he needs food and drink and clothing—essential if a man is to live—he keeps one foot on earth; and all the while he is experiencing the great and abundant joy and sweetness that is in God he has his other foot in eternity. I fancy that this is what St Paul was feeling when he described his great longing. 'Who shall deliver me from this body of death?' (Rom. 7:24) and 'I long to be released and to be with Christ' (Phil. 1:23). So too is it with the soul that experiences Issachar in the affection; it is the joy of interior sweetness that Issachar represents. It strongly urges it to quit this wretched life, which it is quite unable to do. It longs to enter the life of bliss, though it cannot. It does what it can, but it still has to 'live between two extremes'.

VIII

How perfect hatred of sin arises in the affection

Therefore it is *after* Issachar that Zebulon is born: symbolically he stands for *hatred of sin*. We must remind ourselves that hatred of sin is never experienced fully in the affection until a man has known the spiritual joy of interior sweetness. And this is why: until now there has been no real reason for hatred to be felt in the affection. It is the experience of spiritual joy that teaches a man what harms his soul. Once the harm in the soul has been felt, be it much or little, the hatred is proportionate to the damage. But when a soul by the grace of God, and by hard work, has come to know spiritual joy in God, then it realises that sin was the cause which delayed its arrival. So that when a man feels he is not going to persevere in this spiritual joy because of his corrupting flesh—and sin is the cause of this corruption—he develops a strong feeling of hatred against sin of every kind. David said as much in the Psalms, 'Be angry but do not sin.' (4:4.) It means that we are to be angry about sin, but not about nature, for nature prompts deeds, not sins.

We must remember that this anger and hatred is not in opposition to charity. Charity teaches us how it may be had, both in oneself and in one's fellow Christian. For with regard to himself a man ought to hate sin in his own nature, and with regard to his fellow-Christian he ought to hate the sin, but love the sinner. David is thinking of this hatred in the psalm where he says, 'I hated him with perfect hatred'. (139:22.) In another psalm he says he hates all wicked ways. (119:104.)

So it is quite right that Judah and Issachar should be born before Zebulon. For if a man has had love and spiritual joy in his feeling first, it is impossible for him to feel perfect hatred of sin in the affection. Judah, or *charity*, teaches us *how* to hate sin in ourselves and in our fellows: Issachar, *joyful in God*, teaches us *why* we should hate sin. Judah tells us, 'hate sin and love people'; Issachar 'destroy sin and save people'. Thus people are made strong in God and in spiritual things. They really hate sin and destroy it.

It is for this reason that the story describes Zebulon as 'a strong dwelling'. Leah said when he was born, 'My husband shall dwell with me'. God, our true husband, dwells in our soul, and strengthens it with spiritual joy and sweet love in the affection; and that soul earnestly sets about destroying sin, both in himself and others, by utter hatred of it in every form. For this Zebulon was born.

IX

How a proper shame rises and grows in the affection

Although a soul may feel within itself a perfect hatred of sin can it then live without sinning? The answer is 'No'. No man should presume otherwise, since the Apostle has said, 'If we say that we have no sin we deceive ourselves, and the truth is not in us'. (I John 1:8.) St Augustine also says categorically that there is no man who lives without sinning.[1] And who does not sin in ignorance, please? Yes, it often happens that

1. Perhaps in *Ep. ad Hilarium* clvii.

God permits to fall badly those very men by whom he has ordained that other men's errors are to be corrected. By their own falling they learn how merciful they should be in the healing of others. And because men frequently fall into the very sins they most hate, after *hatred of sin* there springs up in the soul *a proper shame*.

And so after Zebulon Dinah is born. Just as Zebulon stands for *hatred of sin* so by Dinah we understand *a proper shame for sin*. But note this: the man who has never experienced Zebulon will never experience Dinah. An evil man has shame of a sort, though it is not a proper shame. Surely if people were really ashamed of sin they would not tolerate it knowingly and deliberately? But their shame is more concerned with the dirty clothes on their body than with the foul thoughts in their soul! If you reckon you have gained Dinah consider this: would you be as much ashamed of the foul thoughts of your heart as you would be to stand naked before the king and the royal court? If the answer is 'no' you can be quite sure that you are not experiencing proper shame, for you are less ashamed of your foul heart than of your filthy body—more ashamed of the body men can see than of the heart which is seen by the king of heaven, his angels and his holy saints!

We have now spoken of the seven children of Leah, and by them we understand seven varieties of affection in a man's soul, which are sometimes lawful, sometimes unlawful, sometimes proper, sometimes improper. When they are lawful and proper they are virtues, when not they become vices. A man must take care that they are both lawful and proper. They are lawful when they are what they ought to be; they are lawless when they are not; and they are proper when they attain their due end, and improper when they go beyond it. For example, too much fear produces despair, too much grief makes a man bitter and depressed and unable to get spiritual comfort. Again, too much hope is presumption; excessive love flatters and cajoles. Too much pleasure makes one dissolute and unruly; intemperate hatred of sin is madness. It is in this way that they are unlawful or improper, and so become vices. They lose the name of 'virtues' and cannot be reckoned among the sons of Jacob—in other words, God. For by 'Jacob' we understand 'God', as we have shown earlier.

C

X

How discretion and contemplation arise in the reason

So it seems that we shall need the virtue of discretion which will govern all the other virtues. Without it every virtue becomes a vice. And he comes! Joseph, born late in time. But his father loves him most of all, for without discretion goodness can neither be attained nor maintained. Small wonder then that this virtue should be particularly loved, for without it no other can be got or governed.

Yet why should we be surprised at the late arrival of this virtue when we cannot acquire perfect discretion without first putting in much practice and hard work on these other qualities? For first of all we must practise each virtue individually and be sure we have got full benefit from them before we can have full knowledge of them all or think clearly about them. And in the process of getting used to these same feelings and insights sometimes we fall down, and as often get up again. It is through our frequent lapses that we learn how careful we have to be in getting and maintaining these virtues. And so, sometimes, through long practice, a soul is led to full discretion, and rejoices then in the birth of Joseph.

Before this virtue was conceived in the soul nothing done by the other virtues was done with discretion. And because a man can presume and force himself with regard to each of these virtues, overtaxing his powers and capacity, so the more seriously can he fall and fail of his purpose. Which is why, last of all, Dinah is born, for hard upon a bad fall and failure comes shame. So, after many falls, many failures, and much shame, a man learns by bitter experience that nothing takes the place of spiritual direction, which is the quickest way of all for achieving discretion. He will never regret anything he does after such advice. For better a wise man than a strong one;[1] yes, and better skill than brute force. It is the wise man who can talk about victory.

And for this reason neither Leah, Zilpah, nor Bilhah could bear such

---

1. Cf. Wisdom 6:1 (Vulgate).

a child, but only Rachel: for, as I have already said, from reason springs sound counsel. Or in other words, *true discretion*, symbolised by Joseph. When we first bring forth Joseph in our reason all that we are moved to do we do with counsel. Joseph not only knows our besetting sin, but he also knows our besetting weakness. And whenever either makes its demand, we apply the remedy and ask counsel of those who are wiser than ourselves, and we do what they say. Else no Josephs are we, no sons of Jacob, born of Rachel.

Moreover, by this same Joseph a man is not only taught to avoid the tricks of his enemies, but often enough he is led on to perfect self-knowledge. And once a man knows himself he can advance in knowing God, whose image and likeness he is. Therefore after Joseph, Benjamin is born; for just as by Joseph we understand discretion, so by Benjamin we understand *contemplation*. They are both born of the same parents. Through the grace of God which enlightens our reason we come to know perfectly both ourselves and God—as far as is possible in this life, of course.

Benjamin is born long after Joseph, for it is true that if we do not apply real effort to this spiritual task (through which we learn to know ourselves), we cannot be raised up to know and contemplate God. He wastes his time who looks up to see God if he cannot first see himself. For I would suggest that before all else a man learns to know the invisible things of his own spirit before he ventures on the invisible things of the spirit of God. He who does not yet know himself, but thinks he has got a fair knowledge of the unseen things of God, is undoubtedly misled. So I advise a man to make it his first business to know himself, made as he is in the image and likeness of God—and that includes his soul.

Be sure of this: he who wants to see God must first cleanse his soul, for it is a mirror which reflects everything clearly if it is clean. When the mirror is dirty you can see nothing clearly. So with the soul: when it is dirty you can neither know yourself nor God. Just as when a candle is burning you can see the candle itself by its own light, and other things too, so when your soul is burning with the love of God, and your heart is feeling a continual desire to love him, then by the light of his grace, which he infuses into your reason, you can see both your unworthiness and his great goodness. Therefore clean your mirror and light your candle. Then when it is clean and burning, and you are aware of the fact, there begins to shine in your soul something of God's light and brightness, and a sunbeam, as it were, appears before your spiritual vision, through which the eye of your soul is opened to behold God and godly things, heaven and heavenly things, and all manner of things spiritual. But this vision is temporary and lasts only for such length of time as God wishes the soul to have on the active service of this mortal life. But in the life to come it will be everlasting.

This was the light that shone in David's soul which he spoke of in the psalm: 'Lord, the light of your countenance is reflected on us. You have put gladness in my heart.' (4:6-7.) The light of God's face is the shining of his grace that forms in us once again his image which had been disfigured by the darkness of sin. Therefore we can be confident that the soul that burns and longs for his light, and hopes to attain it, has conceived its Benjamin. What can be more splendid than this glorious vision? What experience more satisfying? Absolutely nothing! Rachel was perfectly aware of this, for reason tells us that compared with *this* sweetness all sweetness is sour, and bitter as gall compared with honey.

Yet it still remains true that a man cannot attain this grace by his own power. It is the unmerited gift of God. Nevertheless, no man can receive such grace without much prior study and a burning longing. And of that too Rachel was fully aware. So she redoubles her studies and cultivates her longings, each in turn, and at the end of it all, abounding with fervent desire, and deeply sorry that its satisfaction is so delayed, Benjamin is born and his mother Rachel dies. For when a soul is in ecstasy through superabundant longing and immense love, aflame with the light of God, it is surely then that reason dies.

So whoever you may be who are set on contemplating God (or, in other words, on bearing the child called Benjamin, *vision of God*), must do this: you must summon together your thoughts and desires and make of them a church, and within it learn to love only this good word, Jesus. Your whole desire and mind must be set on loving Jesus, without ceasing, as far as possible. In this way you will fulfil the text, 'Lord I will praise you in the church' (Ps. 26:12), that is, in thoughts and desires for the love of Jesus. And then in this 'church' of thought and desire, and in this unity of study and will, make sure that all your thought and desire, all your study and will are directed to love and praise our Lord Jesus, without forgetting, as far as you are able by grace and as your frailty will allow. And always humble yourself to pray and to be directed; waiting patiently on the will of God, until that time when your mind is transported out of itself and fed with splendid food of angels, and you gaze on God, and things to do with him. Then what is written in the psalm will be fulfilled in you, *Ibi Benjamin adolescentus in mentis excessu*,[1] which means in English, 'There is Benjamin, the young child, transported out of mind'.

---

1. Psalm 68:28, Vulgate.

THE
DISCERNMENT
OF
STIRRINGS

A Pistle of Discrecioun of Stirings

THE DISCERNMENT OF STIRRINGS

Introduction

MOST PEOPLE know what it is to have a 'hunch', to have an intuition, or urge, or prompting, to perform some particular action, or to follow a particular course. If they accede to this 'stirring' they are surprised and delighted when their hunch proves right, and they become more sensitive to the next one; but if it does not turn out as they hoped they often become distrustful of such perceptions. Yet even the most susceptible will agree that it is hazardous to live by such impulses, and a sensible person will always 'try the spirits, whether they be of God'. (I John 4:1.)

Christians are no less prone than the non-professing to such inclinations, but in their case the matter becomes more acute. By definition they believe that God can communicate his will to them, often in an heightened awareness of, say, a duty which comes into sharper focus in their consciousness. For them nearly every urge of this sort has to be investigated, and they constantly pray, as in the Collect for Pentecost, for 'a right judgement in all things'.

This is no new phenomenon: the New Testament knew the difficulty and, down through the Desert Fathers, medieval Schoolmen, spiritual masters and mystics, to the present day the same problem exists. Its resolution is always met with the same theological answer. The basic requirement is 'discretion',[1] that virtue which produces the instinctive and right reaction to any situation, which prevents one from ever putting a foot wrong—at least, in the sight of God. It is the fruit of loving him.

In this 'Pistle' the writer is seeking to satisfy his questioner (the same young man to whom *The Cloud* is addressed?) who is worried about his behaviour in varying circumstances. Is he to live by a hard and fast rule,

---

1. 'Discrecioun' is the author's word, and generally we have retained it. 'Discernment' would be in most cases, today's equivalent, though sometimes 'discretion' in our modern sense (namely, freedom to decide at one's own pleasure) would be the better rendering.

never deviating from it, or should he 'play it by ear', and heed the impulse of the moment? How does he acquire this 'discretion'?

The answer given is quite straightforward: he will learn what to do by experience, and the process is never easy. Thus he must acquire in this way a 'parfite knowing of himself and of his inward disposicioun' lest he be deceived. He has got to be humble and ready to accept advice from those more knowledgeable than himself. On no account is he to do things just because he sees other people doing them. He will be constant in prayer, for above and beyond all else he is seeking God in whom he will find all his counsel. The things which are worrying him are relatively unimportant. But union with God means that it is God who is the knowing and acting agent, and in the loving soul he has his instrument. The soul does not lose its identity, however, or its powers of knowing, but now it knows and loves as God knows and loves.

THE DISCERNMENT OF STIRRINGS

A LETTER ABOUT DISTINGUISHING IMPULSES

MY FRIEND IN GOD, the same grace and joy I want for myself I want for you too in the will of God.

You are asking my advice about the relative value of silence and speech, of feeding in general and fasting in particular, of living in community and living in solitude. And you claim to be greatly puzzled about what you should do, for as you say, on the one hand you are considerably hampered by having to speak and feed in common like other folk, and with living communally, yet on the other hand you are afraid to be completely silent, or too strict about fasting, or to live as a solitary, lest you be thought more holy than you are. And there are other dangers beside. For it often happens nowadays that those who are thought very holy can have the most disastrous falls; and it always seems to be those who have been strictest about silence, fasting and solitude.

Grace is essential

But it still remains a fact that they are holy indeed if grace alone has been the cause of their silence and strict fasting and solitary life, their nature but enduring and co-operating in it. Were it to be otherwise there would be real danger from every point of view. For it is extremely risky to submit nature to the strain of such works of devotion (for example, in silence or speech, communal feeding or individual fasting, living in company or alone—I mean, of course, beyond normal custom and capacity), unless one has been led to do so by grace. And led, moreover, to such matters as these which are in themselves unimportant. In other words, they are sometimes good, sometimes bad; sometimes for you, sometimes against; sometimes a help, sometimes a hindrance. It could be that were you always to follow the particular urge that would bind you to silence, strict fasting and solitude, you would often be dumb when you ought to be speaking, fasting when you ought to be eating, and on your own when you should be with others. Alternatively, if you spoke whenever you liked, and ate and lived with people, then perhaps you would speak when you ought to be quiet, and feed when you should be fasting, and keep company when the occasion called for solitude. And you could so easily go wrong, to the great confounding not only of your own soul, but of others' also. Therefore, to avoid such mistakes, you ask me (if I read your letter aright) two things: first, my opinion of you and these impulses of yours, and, second, my advice on the matter, and on all other things as they arise.

The knowledge which brings peace

As to the first, my answer is that in matters of this kind I am loath to put forward my own opinion (such as it is) for two reasons. The first is this: I dare not rely on my own view and assert that it is absolutely true; the other is that your inner make-up and your capacity for all the things your letter speaks of is not as well known to me as it ought to be if I am to give you adequate advice. For, as the Apostle says, *Nemo novit quae sunt hominis nisi spiritus hominis qui in ipso est*. No one knows the secret temperament of a man but the spirit of that man himself. (I Cor. 2:11.)

And maybe you yourself do not yet know your own inner character as well as you will one day, when God has let you prove it through many fallings and risings. I have never yet known a sinner come to a perfect knowledge of himself and his basic temperament without having been taught it in the school of God, by the experience of many temptations and frequent stumblings and risings. For just as through the waves and floods and storms of the sea, and through the gentle wind and calm and fair weather as well, the frail ship finally makes landfall and reaches port, so through the varied temptations and tribulations that befall a soul in the ups and downs of life (the floods and storms of the sea), and through the grace and goodness of the Holy Spirit, with his frequent visits, sweetness, and spiritual strengthening (the gentle and fair weather), the frail soul, like the ship, reaches firm land and the haven of salvation. To put it in other words, one comes to a clear and honest understanding of oneself and all one's inner motives. Once he has this knowledge a man may sit at peace with himself, like some crowned king over his realm, in firm, intelligent and proper control of himself, his thoughts and his impulses, physical and spiritual.

The crown of life

It is of such that the wise man speaks, *Beatus vir qui suffert temptationem, quoniam cum probatus fuerit accipiet coronam vitae, quam repromisit Deus diligentibus se.* Blessed is the man that endures temptation, for when he has been proved he will receive the crown of life which God has promised to all who love him. (James 1:12.)

'The crown of life' can be understood in two ways: (i) Spiritual wisdom, discernment, and perfection of virtue. Together these three can be called a crown of life which, helped by grace, we may attain in this present life. (ii) A second meaning can be attached to it: it is the endless joy that every true soul shall have after this life in the bliss of heaven. Indeed, a man cannot receive either of these crowns until he has been well tested by hardship and temptation. As the text says, *Quoniam cum probatus fuerit, accipiet coronam vitae,* when he has been proved he will receive the crown of life. And as I understand it (and have said before), this is saying that unless a sinner has first been tested by various trials, now rising up, now falling down (falling through weakness, rising by grace), he can never receive in this life from God (i) spiritual wisdom and clear understanding of himself and his inner temperament, nor (ii) discernment so necessary to teach and counsel others, nor (iii) the perfection of virtue, which consists in loving God and his brother.

All three of these (wisdom, discernment, perfection of virtue) are one, and may be called the 'crown of life'. There are three things in a crown,[1] gold, precious stones, and the 'turrets' of the fleur-de-lis which project beyond the head. I understand 'gold' to represent *wisdom*, 'precious stones' *discernment*, and the 'fleur-de-lis turrets' *perfection of virtue*. Gold encircles the head, and by wisdom we control our every

---

1. The crown, to the author, was not the heavy confection now worn by British monarchs, but something much simpler. Basically it was a flat band of gold encircling the head from the upper edge of which projected five (or three, the experts are not agreed) fleur-de-lis, the French symbol of monarchy. The England of the fourteenth century was still much influenced by France.

kind of spiritual activity. Precious stones help us to see men by their light, and through our ability to discern we instruct and advise our brothers. The turrets of the fleur-de-lis have two sprigs, one branching out on the right side and one on the left, and a third sprig which goes straight up above its head. By perfection of virtue, or charity, we spread out two side branches of love, on the right to our friends, on the left to our enemies; and there is a third which goes straight up to God, above man's understanding, the head of the soul. This is the crown of life which, by grace, we may obtain here below.

So conduct yourself modestly in your fight, and endure your temptations humbly until you have been proved. For once proved you shall receive either the one crown here and the other crown hereafter, or else indeed both of them here and afterwards. For he who has his crown here can be sure of the other hereafter. There are very many who through grace have been proved here below and yet have never attained what could have been theirs in this life. If they humbly persevere and await God's will with patience they will receive in full abundance that other crown in the bliss of heaven. You think the crown that may be had here beautiful? Yes, indeed, but accept humbly through grace that compared with the crown there it is no more than a pound note in a world full of gold. I say all this to comfort and encourage you in the spiritual fight you are waging through your faith in our Lord.

The necessity for examining impulses

And, too, I say all this to show you how far you still are from a real knowledge of yourself, and to warn you not to give up too soon, and not to follow the special impulses of your youthful heart for fear of being deceived. Moreover, I say all this to let you see what I am thinking about you and your impulses as you have asked me to do. For my opinion is that you are quite capable of, and indeed eager for, sudden impulses to do particular things, and quick to hold on to them once you get them—and that is a very dangerous thing!

I am not saying that this ability and eagerness of yours, or any other similar inclination, is, for all its danger, therefore evil in itself. No, I am saying nothing of the kind. What I am saying is that potentially it can be a good thing, and a very great help to very great perfection;

yes, and to the greatest possible perfection in this life. But that can only be if a soul so disposed will diligently, day and night, humble itself before God and take sound advice; if it will take steps to offer itself up; if it will give up its own mind and will in these sudden, special impulses and state categorically that it will not follow them, however attractive, uplifting and holy they may be, unless it has the full approval of its spiritual masters, those who have been long experienced in the solitary life. Such a soul, who continues humbly in this way, may well deserve, through grace and its own taste of spiritual conflict, to receive the crown of life already mentioned.

And great as is the capacity for good in one who, as I say, has this humble disposition, so equally it can be very dangerous in another soul, in one who suddenly, without warning or advice, follows the impulses of its eager heart, according to its own ideas and will. So for the love of God beware of this capacity and the sort of inclination I am speaking of, if you have it as I suggest. Humbly and continually give yourself to prayer and counsel. Crush your own ideas and will in these sudden, special urges, and do not follow them unheedingly, until you have found out where they come from, and whether they are for you or against you.

About these impulses on which you ask my advice and opinion: I must say that I view them all with suspicion, for fear they are being conceived in a way I call ape-like. It is often said that the ape copies whatever he sees others do. Do please forgive me if I am wrong in this suspicion! Nevertheless, the love I have for your soul prompts me to it as does the evidence that reaches me through a spiritual brother who is both yours and mine. He was recently in your area, and was touched by the same promptings as yourself towards strict silence, rigorous fasts, and complete solitude—'like an ape', he admitted to me at the end of a long conversation, and after he had examined himself and his impulses. For, as he said, he had seen a man in your district who, as is well known, observes a great silence, performs extraordinary fasts, and lives in solitude. I have no doubt whatever that the man in question has received true and real promptings, and that they have been through grace alone, experienced within himself, and not by anything he has seen or heard of another's silence. Had it been otherwise it could be called ape-like, as I am trying to say.

So beware, and thoroughly examine your impulses and their sources. For *how* you have been prompted, whether within by grace or without in ape fashion, only God knows, not I. Nevertheless I can say this to you so that you can avoid such: 'Make sure you are no ape!' That is to say, see that your impulses to silence or speech, fasting or eating, solitude or company, come from within out of an abundant love and devotion of spirit, and not from outside through the windows of your bodily senses, your ears and your eyes. For, as Jeremiah says plainly, *Mors entrat per fenestras*—'Death enters by such windows'. (9:21.) For all its inadequacy this is enough, I think, to answer your first request, which asks my opinion of you and the impulses of which you speak in your letter.

Jesus, the Angel of Great Counsel

With regard to the second matter on which you ask my advice, in this case and others like it, I ask almighty Jesus, 'the Angel of Great Counsel' (Isaiah 9:6), that in his mercy he will be your counsellor and comforter in all your distress and need. Through his wisdom may he guide me to fulfil, at any rate in part—for my teaching is very simple— the heartfelt trust you place in me rather than in any other person. In me, simple, ignorant and wretched me, not fit to teach you or anybody else because of my little grace and less skill! All the same, for all my ignorance, I will still say something in response to your desire for my simple knowledge. I trust that God's grace will teach and lead when natural and theological knowledge fail.

You know well enough that in themselves, whether we consider them collectively or individually, none of these things (silence, speech, fasting, eating, solitude or company) is the true end of our desire. But for some men—not for all—they are the means towards the end if they are done lawfully and sensibly. Otherwise they hinder more than they help. So I think I will not give you definite advice at this time when to speak or be still, to eat or fast, to mix or to live alone, for perfection does not depend on these. But I will give some general advice to hold on to when you have impulses like these, and come up against two opposites such as silence and speech, fasting and eating, solitude and company, the normal clothes of ordinary Christians and the particular habits[1] of different and distinct brotherhoods. Whatever other such distinctions there be, in themselves they are but the work of nature and of men.

For you know both by instinct and by the rules of polite behaviour when to speak and when to be quiet, when to eat and when to fast, when to mix and when to be alone, when to wear ordinary clothes and when a particular habit. And you have this knowledge whenever you want it, and whenever you see that some of it might be useful and helpful in nourishing the heavenly grace at work in your soul. God forbid that you or anyone else should be so stupid and blinded by the sorry temptations of that devil that 'destroyeth in the noonday' (cf. Ps. 91:7) as to bind yourself by some false vow to any peculiar practice under the guise of a holiness pretended in the spirit of pious servitude. It will destroy, completely and finally, the freedom of Christ which is the spiritual habit worn by utter holiness, whether in this life or the next. Witness St Paul: *Ubi spiritus Domini, ubi libertas.* Where the Spirit of the Lord is, there is freedom. (II Cor. 3:17.)

So when you see that all such works in practice can be both good and bad I beg you to leave both well alone. It is the most sensible thing to do if you would be humble. Leave off your inquisitive investigations, trying to find out which is better. Rather do this: put one on this side and the other on that, and then choose something between them. When you have done this you are free to accept or reject either of them, whenever you like and without blame.

The necessity for a loving choosing of God

But, of course, you ask me what that 'something' is. I will tell you what I mean. It is God, for whose sake you are quiet if you should be quiet; for whose sake you speak if you have to speak; for whose sake you fast if you ought to fast; for whose sake you eat if that is right for you; for whose sake you live alone if that is what you ought to do; for whose sake you mix with people if you are to keep company; and so on, whatever it is.

---

1. 'Habits': not what they do, of course, but what they wear.

For silence is not God, nor speaking; fasting is not God, nor eating; solitude is not God, nor company; nor any other pair of opposites. He is hidden between them, and cannot be found by anything your soul does, but only by the love of your heart. He cannot be known by reason, he cannot be thought, caught, or sought by understanding. But he can be loved and chosen by the true, loving will of your heart. Then choose him, and you will speak by your silence, and there will be silence in your speech; you will be fasting while you eat, and eating when you fast; and so for the rest.

This loving choosing of God springs from the pure intention of a true heart, and looks for him, wisely and freely, between all such pairs, and when they come holds on to neither, but offers them up as the aim and object of our spiritual gazing. It is the most worthwhile seeking and searching for God that can be attained or learnt in this life—I mean for a contemplative soul. Yes, even though that soul in its search sees nothing that can be understood by the spiritual eye of its reason. For if God is your love and your purpose, the chief aim of your heart, it is all you need in this life, although you never see more of him with the eye of reason your whole life long. Such a blind shot with the sharp dart of longing love will never miss its mark, which is God. He himself says as much in the Book of Love when he speaks to the languishing, loving soul, *Vulnerasti cor meum, soror mea, amica mea, sponsa mea, vulnerasti cor meum in uno oculorum tuorum.* 'You have wounded my heart, my sister, my beloved, my spouse, you have wounded my heart with but one of your eyes.'[1] The eyes of the soul are two, reason and love. Reason enables us to see how mighty, how wise, and how good he is in his creation, but not in himself. But whenever reason fails, then love is eager to live and learn to play its full part. For by love we may find him, feel him, and catch him just as he is. It is a wonderful eye, love, for the loving soul says to our Lord, 'You have wounded my heart with but one of your eyes', meaning that love which is blind to everything else but the one thing it is seeking. This is why it finds and feels and hits and wounds the target it is shooting at much sooner than it would had its glance ranged over many things—as for example when

1. Canticles 4:9 (Vulgate).

reason goes rummaging and looking among things as varied as silence, speech, fasting, eating, solitude, company, seeking which is the better.

One thing is needful

Give up these preoccupations, I beg you, and ignore them as if you did not know such things existed—I mean as ways of reaching God. Truly there is no other way if you will be really contemplative, and attain your purpose swiftly. So with the apostle I beg you and all like you, *Videte vocationem vestram, et in ea vocatione quae vocati estis, state.* Look to your calling, and in that calling to which you have been called, stand firm and stand fast in the name of Jesus.[1] Your calling is to be a true contemplative like Mary, Martha's sister. Then do what Mary did. *Porro unum est necessarium,* one thing is necessary (Luke 10:42), so make the object of your heart one thing: God. Him you want, him you seek, him you long to love, him you long to feel, him you long to clasp—and by none of those things, silence, speech, fasting, feasting, solitude, society. For sometimes silence is good, but at the same time it were better to speak; again, sometimes it is speaking that is good, but silence better, and so for all the rest, fasting, eating, solitude, company, and suchlike. Sometimes one is good but the other is better, but neither of them is at any time the best. So let all that is good be good, and all that is better be better, for both are going to cease and come to an end. See yourself as Mary, and choose the best which will never fail. *Maria (inquit optimus) optimam partem elegit, quae non auferetur ab ea.* The best is Almighty Jesus, and he said that Mary, type of all contemplatives, had chosen the best which would never be taken from her. So I beg you, with Mary, leave the good and the better, and choose the best.

Let go, then, of such things as silence, speech, fasting, eating, solitude and company and so on; don't bother about them. You do not know what they signify, and I beg you not to try to find out. If ever you have to think or speak of them, say that they are such high and admirable matters of perfection (knowing how and when to speak, or be silent, to fast or to eat, to be alone or in company), that it would be

1. A conflation of I Cor. 1:26, 7:20, Eph. 4:1 and 6:13.

folly and presumption for a weak wretch like yourself to dabble in such great perfection. For all these things are natural things, but how and when to do them can be known only through grace.

And undoubtedly such grace is never got by the sort of strict silence or special fasting or solitude that you are speaking of, for these originate from outside, through hearing and seeing other people do them. But if ever this grace is to be had, it must come from within, and be learned from God; and for him you have eagerly longed for many a day with all the love of your heart. For whose sake too you have utterly eliminated from your soul's vision all consideration of anything less than himself—though some of the things I have bid you put away might seem in the eyes of some people effective ways of reaching God. Yes, let them say what they will; just do as I bid you, the result will speak for itself. For to him who is eager to achieve his spiritual purpose it is a sufficient method; he needs no more than the actual thought of God, with a reverent urge of lasting love. Your only means of reaching God is God himself. But you must keep intact that movement of love which you experience in your heart by grace, and not let your spiritual gaze stray from it.

The outcome is discernment

Then that very thing you are experiencing will know how to tell you when to speak and when to be silent. It will govern your whole life with discretion and certainty, and will teach you mystically how to begin and how to cease in all these natural matters with great and supreme wisdom. For if by grace you are able to keep it in use and continual practice, then, whether you have to speak or eat or live in the company of other people, or to do any other such things that are normal and natural to Christians, it will first quietly prompt you to speak or to do the right and natural thing, whatever it is. But if you do not do it, it will strike you hard and prick your conscience and give you no peace till you do. Similarly, were you to be speaking or doing some quite normal thing, when properly you ought to be engaged in something quite different (as different as fasting is from eating, solitude from company, and so on—all works of individual holiness) then it will urge you to do it.

36

So it is by the experience of this blind movement of love to God that a contemplative soul comes most quickly to that grace of discernment which knows when to speak and when to be quiet, when to eat and when to fast, when to mix and when to be alone, and so on. It comes more quickly than by any of the particular schemes you mention, whether arising from the inner activity of one's own thought and will or from the outside example of others' doings of every kind. Such strenuous activity prompted by nature and not by grace is a temporary affliction and quite useless! Its only use is for religious, or for those on whom some penance has been laid; the profit then is not because of the exertion, but because of the obedience which prompted it. Without that it is merely painful to those who undergo it. But lovingly and eagerly to want to have God is great, surpassing comfort and true spiritual peace, and a foretaste of eternal joy.

The truth shall make you free

Therefore speak when you like and cease when you like; eat when you like and fast when you like; mix when you like and be alone when you like, so that God and his grace can lead you. Let him fast who wants to and be alone if he wishes; let him keep silence too if he so desires. But you must hold on to God who plays no one false. For silence, speech, fasting, eating, solitude and company—all these can mislead you. If you should hear of any man who speaks, or of any that is silent; of any that eats, or of any fasting; of anyone who enjoys company, or who keeps to himself, think to yourself, and say it out aloud if necessary, that they know what they ought to do—unless of course the truth is plainly otherwise. But see that you do not as they do (I mean because they do it and you ape them), for you cannot do it nor, probably, are your inclinations theirs. Therefore stop working to other men's specifications, and work according to your own, so long as you know what they are! And until such time, take the advice of people who do know what they are about, though you need not follow their particular inclinations. Such men should give *advice* in such cases, and nothing else. This is enough answer to your letter.

The grace of God be always with you, in the name of Jesus. Amen.

THE
DISCERNING
OF
SPIRITS

A Tretis of Discrescyon of Spirites

THE DISCERNING OF SPIRITS

Introduction

THIS TREATISE is commonly regarded as the slightest of the *Cloud* writings, and in the sense that it deals with the ascetic rudiments of the spiritual life rather than with its fuller development, such a view is justified. But for precisely the same reason it remains a document of considerable importance for the whole series.

The writer makes use of two sermons of St Bernard[1] which he freely translates, adapts and rearranges to serve his own purpose. These take up one third of the tract, but have been worked in so skilfully that the reader is unaware of the borrowings.

The main purpose is to help the contemplative in his battle against evil by enabling him to distinguish between his own spirit and the different hostile spirits intent on dragging him down to hell. Of these the world, the flesh and the devil are all three thoroughly bad, but the third is supremely so, and is always singled out as 'that spirit of malice, wrath and wickedness', the quintessence of all that is evil. Though, alas, a soul may embroil itself in sin, and seem indistinguishable from a devil, it is always potentially salvable, and almost casually the writer drops hints, when he is not being more specific, as to the means whereby the power of the Fiend may be overcome. Fundamentally it has to be through the presence of God, with his gifts of peace and restfulness of heart. The confidence this brings, together with a certain amount of skill in discerning the foe's devices, and with the aid of grace, determination, prayer and counsel, will thwart all attacks and keep the spiritual head above water. But 'counsel' is given primarily in sacramental confession, and implies the existence of an experienced director whose advice and guidance are essential. More is written here (though it is little enough) than anywhere else in these writings on this basic subject.

Through the use of these means the contemplative will acquire the

---

1. *Sermones de Diversis* xxiii and xxiv. St Bernard is responsible to a greater or less degree for paragraphs i-iv, viii-xi and xvi and for this reason paragraph numbers have been inserted.

the ability to distinguish his own human response from the three-fold source of temptation. This is important, for it will allay the morbidity and danger that await a soul who thinks all temptation is sin, and does not discern between what must be avoided and what must be overcome.

THE DISCERNING OF SPIRITS

BECAUSE there are varieties of spirits, it is necessary that we should be able to distinguish between them for, as St John has taught us, we are not to believe all spirits (I John 4:1). It might seem to some, especially those unskilled in spiritual matters, that every thought that sounds in man's heart is spoken by man's own spirit and by no other. That this is not the case both our Faith and the witness of the Bible clearly demonstrate: 'I shall listen', says the prophet David, 'not to what I myself say, but to whatever my Lord God will speak inside me.' (Ps. 85:8.) Another prophet says that an angel spoke in him (Zech. 1:9). Also, the Psalms teach us that wicked spirits send evil thoughts into men's hearts (78:49). Moreover, that there is a carnal spirit (and not a good one), the Apostle Paul clearly shows when he talks of some men 'vainly puffed up with their fleshly spirit' (Col. 2:18). And he also makes it plain that there is a spirit of the world, in the passage where he rejoices in God, not only for himself but for his disciples as well, that they had not received the spirit of the world, but that which was sent from God, the Holy Spirit (I Cor. 2:12).

ii These two spirits (of the flesh and the world) are servants or attendants, as it were, of that cursed spirit, the foul Fiend of hell, and this spirit of wickedness is the lord of them both. We are to believe none of these three spirits when they speak to us, because they never speak without hurt to body and soul.

How to distinguish the three evil spirits

iii We can identify whichever spirit is speaking to us by what it says. The fleshly spirit always speaks in terms of creature comfort; the worldly spirit of things to do with possessions and pomp; the fiendish spirit of things cruel and bitter. And whenever our minds turn to food or drink, or sleep or dress, or lust, and so on—all things that have to do with the flesh—and our hearts burn with a desire and longing for such things, we can be quite sure that it is the spirit of flesh that is speaking.

So we put him away as best we can, with the help of grace, for he is our enemy. And whenever we think of the empty joy of this world, which makes us want to be well esteemed and favoured, to possess great breeding and knowledge, to be reckoned wise and worthy, to have high standing and office—ideas which would make a man seem big and important in others' eyes, and in his own as well—there can be no doubt that it is the spirit of the world that is thus speaking, a far more dangerous enemy than that of the flesh, and much more difficult to put away.

The Fiend of hell

iv It often happens that these two servants and assistants of the foul Fiend, spirit and prince of wrath and wickedness, are firmly put down and trampled under foot by grace and a soul's skill. But sometimes it is the cunning of their malicious master, the foul Fiend of hell, who slyly withdraws them as part of his plan to rise up with great and malevolent wrath, like a lion on the rampage, and attack our sick and helpless souls. And this occurs when our heart moves us, not to physical lust or to empty, worldly pleasure, but to grumbling and complaint, to grief, bitterness and pain, to impatience, wrath, melancholy, evil will, to hatred, envy and all such sorry matters. It tends to 'get us down' if things are done or said to us less lovingly or wisely than we would wish. Evil suspicions begin to arise. If anything is suggested by gesture or expression, word or deed, if it can somehow be made malicious or depressing, it at once makes us so interpret it.

v These thoughts and others like them destroy our fundamental peace and quiet, and we must resist them no less firmly than we resist the very Fiend of hell; we must flee from them as vigorously as we would from the loss of our soul. There can be no doubt that the spirits of these thoughts, both carnal and worldly, are working and striving in every possible way to procure the loss of our soul, but the greatest danger is from the Fiend himself. For he can do this on his own, but not they without him. Be a soul never so free from carnal lust and worldly vanity, if it is corrupted by this spirit of malice, wrath and wickedness, it will probably perish, notwithstanding it is clean in all other respects. And be a soul never so corrupted by carnal and worldly lust and pleasure, by grace it may yet keep itself in peace and quiet with regard to its fellow Christians—though this is hard enough given the continuing habits of these other two!—and will less probably be lost, despite the filth already referred to.

vi So although the lustful thoughts of our foul flesh are evil and the empty pleasure of the world is even worse, I call this bitter thing, this spirit of malice, wrath and wickedness, the worst spirit of them all. Why? The first steals devotion from the soul; the second robs us of the true joy we should experience when we contemplate heavenly things, brought us and taught us by the very angels; but the third takes from us the best of all: charity, in other words, God. (And, indeed, those who are so anxious to be honoured, favoured and waited on by their fellow men deserve to miss the honour, favour and attention that angels bring them here below whenever they contemplate the things of heaven. For contemplation of this sort is in itself better and more worthwhile even than the desire for and enjoyment of devotion.)

The presence and the peace of God

vii For he who lacks peace and restfulness of heart lacks also the living presence and the loving prospect of the supreme peace of heaven, good and gracious God, his own dear self. This is what David declares in the psalms, when he says that the tabernacle of God is made in peace, and his dwelling is in Zion (132:14, 76:2). Zion symbolises the vision of peace. And the soul's 'sight' is the same as the soul's 'thought'. Certainly in the soul that is most occupied with peaceful thoughts God has made his dwelling-place. God himself says as much when he speaks by the prophet, 'Upon whom does my spirit rest, if not upon the humble and quiet?' (Is. 66:2.)

The wiles of the devil

viii So he who would have God continually within him, and live in love, experiencing the supreme peace of God—the greatest and best part of contemplation possible in this life—must see to it day and night that he puts down, whenever they come, the spirit of the flesh and the spirit of the world, and, above all, the spirit of malice, wrath and wickedness, the most foul and filthy of the lot. It is most necessary and useful to know his craftiness, and not be ignorant of his miserable deceits. For sometimes this wicked, cursed creature changes his appearance into that of an angel of light so that he, under the colour of virtue, can do more harm. It is then but the seed of bitterness and discord he is demonstrating, however holy and fair it looks at first sight.

ix He leads a great many into unusual sanctity, well beyond the normal practices and principles of their calling, as for example in the matter of fasts, clothes and many other devout observances and external customs, so that they openly reprove the shortcomings of others—which have nothing to do with them. Things like these, and many others, he moves them to do, all under the cloak of devotion and charity. Not that he rejoices in such, but because he loves dissension and slander, which are always provoked by unseemly individualism. For wherever in any devout congregation there are one or two people who go in for such peculiarities, then, as the fool sees it, all the rest are behaving scandalously. But in the eyes of the wise it is *they* who cause scandal. But since there are more fools than sensible people, their influence is such that these individualists reckon they are wise, whereas, if they only realised it, they and their fellows should be shown up to be the fools they are and would see the devil's darts, meant to destroy simple souls under the pretence of salvation and love. The Fiend employs many such tricks. But the man who refuses to consent, and submits humbly to prayer and counsel, by the grace of God will be free from all these wiles.

The slavery of sin

x Sad to say, and even sadder to know, our own spirit is sometimes overcome by these three spirits of the world, the flesh and the Devil. At such a time it is in grave danger, bound and tied, subjected and enslaved by all of them. It is a sorry thing to know, that in the great confusion and loss it brings upon itself, it can now only do what each of the three wants of it. It is the result of long-standing and habitual acquiescence in their suggestions, so that the soul ultimately becomes so carnal, worldly and malicious, so wicked and perverse, that of its own accord, with no outside prompting, it breeds and bears not only lustful, carnal thoughts and empty, worldly ones, but, worst of all, the bitter, wicked thoughts which are cantankerous, critical and mischievous.

xi And when this happens to us it is not always easy to know when it is our own spirit that is speaking, or when we are hearing one of the three other spirits speaking through it. But what does it matter who is speaking when it is one and the same thing that is spoken? What help is it to know which person is speaking when it is quite certain that all that is being said is evil and dangerous? If it is your enemy, do not yield to him, but humbly turn to prayer and counsel; in this way you may powerfully withstand him. If it is your own spirit, rebuke him sharply and with sorrowful sighs repent that you ever fell into so great wretchedness, slavery and servitude. Confess your habitual acquiescence and your long-standing sins; by grace you may be able to recover your freedom again.

Discerning the spirits

xii By this gracious freedom you may quickly come to know in your own experience when your own spirit is uttering these evil things, and when they are the evil spirits speaking through you. This knowledge can become the greatest help in resisting them. For ignorance is often at the back of error; equally, knowledge can promote truth. May you come to this way of knowing as I describe it to you! If you are uncertain or in doubt about these evil spirits when they come, whether it is you or they who are speaking, take a quick look at what your counsellor and your conscience tell you. Have you, according to your confessor's directions, been absolved from, and done penance for, all those times that you yielded to that particular sin you are aware of? If not, then make your confession as truthfully as you can, after taking counsel and by God's grace. Then you can be quite sure that all thoughts that come after your absolution, prompting you to the same sins, are what other spirits are telling you; they are not your own. I mean, of course, one of the three I have mentioned. Thereafter you will be blameable for none of those thoughts when they come, however many and foul they may be unless, indeed, you are careless about resisting them. But if you firmly resist them, you may expect not merely release from the purgatory you deserve for whatever sins you have committed, but also may have much grace in this life here, and much reward in the bliss of heaven.

Training the conscience

xiii But all those evil thoughts which come to you, moving you to sin, to which you consented and before you repented of your consent and wanted to be shriven, you can, without harm, take to yourself and seek to be rid of them as if they were your own thoughts. But to take responsibility for all those other thoughts which you have proved to be the thoughts of other spirits than yourself—therein lies great danger. You could so easily mislead your conscience, accounting a thing sinful when it is nothing of the kind. This is a great mistake and could lead to very real danger. For were each evil thought and inclination the work of man's own spirit only, it would follow that this spirit was a devil, and this is clearly false and damnable nonsense. Although a soul, through its weakness and sinful habits, may fall into such wretchedness and bondage that it takes over the work of the Devil, urging itself on to sin after sin without any fiendish prompting, it is not for that reason a devil by nature. It is a devil in functon, however, and can be called devilish, since its actions are like the Devil's. Yet for all its enslavement to sin and to devilry, by grace it may, through contrition, confession and amendment, recover its freedom again and be saved— yes, and become one of God's special saints here in this life, even though once it had been under sentence and the curse.

xiv And great as the danger is for a sinner not to charge his conscience with it, nor to amend his ways, it is just as dangerous and (perhaps one could say) even more so, for a man to charge his conscience with every one of the sinful thoughts and temptations which come to him. For by such folly he might easily run into error and despair all his life. And the reason would be that he did not know how to discern spirits, a knowledge which comes through first-hand experience, and is given to him who, as I have said earlier, takes that 'quick look' as soon as his soul has been cleansed by confession.

Freedom to choose

xv For immediately after confession, a soul is, as it were, a clean sheet of paper in that it is able to receive whatever people want to write on it. On the soul made clean by confession God and his angels strive to write; so too do the Fiend and his angels. But the soul is free to choose whichever it wants; it gets what it consents to. That new thought and prompting to sin, which you recently forsook in your confession, what is it but one of the three spirits—the enemies I have spoken of—trying to write the same sin on your soul again? It is not you who speaks thus, for there is nothing of the kind written on your soul: it has all been washed away in your confession. Your soul is naked and bare, with nothing beyond a frail, but free, ability to consent. Maybe it is more inclined to its accustomed evil than to goodness, but at the same time more able to be good than to be evil, because of its cleanness of soul and the power of sacramental confession. But of itself there is nothing whereby it can think or urge itself to good or ill. Therefore it follows that whatever thought comes to it, good or evil, does not come from the soul. But its consent to good or evil, whichever it is, is always the work of the same soul.

xvi According to the worth or wretchedness of this consent, so is measured the pain or bliss. If the consent is to evil, then at once, by such association, it takes over the function of the very spirit that suggested it in the first instance. If it is to the good, then at once it has, by grace, the same function as the spirit that first prompted it. For as often as a wholesome thought comes into our minds (for example, chastity, seriousness, rejection of the world, voluntary poverty, patience, humility, love) there can be no doubt but that it is the spirit of God that is speaking to us, either directly or through one of his angels—angels in this life who teach us truth, or angels in glory who are the real instigators and inspirers of goodness.

The work of the soul

xvii A soul, through long practice and habitual consent to the three evil spirits, can become so carnal, worldly and malicious that it can be said to take over the functions of them all. On the other hand, a soul which habitually does good can become so spiritual through clean living and resistance to the flesh, so heavenly-minded in dealing with the spirit of the world, and so godly through peace and love and inner quiet when faced with the spirit of malice, wrath and wickedness, that it has the ability to think all such good thoughts whenever it likes, and to keep them perfectly in mind, subject always to the limitations of this life.

Christian Spirituality